cocktails

the perfect guide to cocktail making **STEP-BY-STEP**

cocktails

the perfect guide to cocktail making **STEP-BY-STEP**

LOVE FOOD™

First published in 2012
LOVE FOOD is an imprint of Parragon Books Ltd

Parragon
Queen Street House
4 Queen Street
Bath BA1 1HE, UK

ISBN: 978-1-4454-8283-5

Printed in China

Cover design by Geoff Borin
Internal design by Talking Design
Introduction by Paul Martin
Edited by Fiona Biggs

Notes for the Reader
This book uses standard kitchen measuring spoons and cups. All spoon and cup measurements
are level unless otherwise indicated. Unless otherwise stated, milk is assumed to be whole
and eggs are large. Recipes using raw eggs should be avoided by infants, the elderly,
pregnant women, convalescents and anyone suffering from an illness. Please consume alcohol
responsibly.

contents

introduction

This beautiful book with its delightful recipes and enticing photography will quickly become an indispensable tool for any budding mixologist. In this comprehensive collection, you'll find punches for parties, short drinks for unwinding in the evening, and impressive crowd-pleasers for entertaining. All recipes are simply written to make them easy to follow and will guarantee even the novice cocktail maker a winning result every time.

Cocktails have played a colorful part in modern history and have cemented their place in popular culture. The history of the first cocktails remains a mystery, and this has led to a number of popular folk tales. One of the more popular stories that's been told recounts how, during the Revolutionary War, American and French soldiers frequented Betsy's tavern to enjoy a famous alcoholic concoction of her own design, known as "Betsy's Bracer." One night, amid wild drinking and parties, one of the American soldiers stole a couple of roosters from a neighbor's yard. He toasted his theft with his drinking companions, saying "Here's to the divine liquor, which is as delicious to the palate as the cock's tail is beautiful to the eye," to which a French officer is said to have responded "Vive le Cocktail!"—and with that, the term "cocktail" was apparently born!

Since their conception, cocktails have seen trends come and go—from the days of the practical cocktail (when mixers were used to disguise the flavors of homemade liquor during the Prohibition), to the fancy, frivolous cocktails favored in the 1980s, to the pared-back, stylish cocktails made famous by stage and screen characters in the early years of this century.

Why you need this book
The art of the skilled mixologist is based on a set of easy-to-follow principles that can put almost anyone on the right track to producing an extensive range of cocktails and mixed drinks. In this book, all the necessary skills are explained in layman's terms, allowing the reader to effortlessly apply them to the broad range of featured cocktail recipes. Simply read up on the terminology and techniques that follow and get started on the recipes—and soon you'll be mixing and shaking with the best of them.

mixing methods

Creating a cocktail is not brain surgery, but it does require the deft touch of a skilled mixologist. Follow the measurements in the recipe, because these are balanced for the best flavor. A standard jigger or shot glass holds 1½ ounces, which is equivalent to 3 tablespoons. A pony shot glass holds only 1 ounce. The better your mixing techniques, the finer the quality of the resulting drink. There are several mixing methods, all of which have benefits behind their recommended usage. The following are the most commonly used methods and the ones to be found within these pages.

> **Shaking:** This is when we add all the ingredients, with a scoop of ice, to the cocktail shaker and then shake vigorously for approximately 5 seconds. The benefit of shaking is that the drink is rapidly mixed, chilled, and aerated—you will notice that after the drink has been shaken, the outside of the shaker itself will be lightly frosted. Shaking a cocktail will also dilute the drink significantly.

>1 >2 >3

>1 >2 >3

This dilution is a necessary part of the process and gives shaken recipes the requisite balance of taste, strength, and temperature.

In addition, we may also choose to shake a drink that includes an ingredient, such as egg white, that would not combine effectively with a less vigorous form of mixing.

> **Stirring:** With this technique, we once again add all the ingredients to a scoop of ice, but this time combine them in a mixing glass or small pitcher. We then stir the ingredients together using a long-handled bar spoon.

As with the shaken method, this allows us to blend and chill the ingredients but, unlike the shaken method, the erosion of the ice is significantly less and consequently we are able to control the level of dilution and keep it to a minimum. This simple but vital technique is essential for a number of drinks that do not require much dilution, such as a classic Dry Martini.

> **Building:** To "build" a drink, we simply make it in the glass, as you would with a gin and tonic. It is important to follow the instructions for built cocktails because the order of ingredients can change from drink to drink and this can impact upon the flavors.

> **Muddling:** We muddle ingredients when we are trying to extract juice or oils from the pulp or

skin of a fruit, herb, or spice. A muddler is simply a pestle that we would use to crush the ingredient accordingly—you can get a specific tool for the job or, alternatively, use a wooden rolling pin.

> **Blending:** As the name suggests, this is when the ingredients are combined in a blender! The goal for most blended drinks is that they are served with a smooth consistency. Accordingly, the ingredients are usually blended with a scoop of crushed ice and

>4 >5 >6

often include items, such as fresh fruit, that can't be shaken or stirred.

> **Layering:** When creating layers in a cocktail, it's important to follow the instructions, because the heavier liquors or liqueurs must go into the glass first.

The first, base layer should be poured into the center of the glass, without getting any down the sides, if possible. To create the second layer, we turn a teaspoon upside down, with the tip touching the inside of the glass and pour the liquid slowly over the back of the spoon (moving it up the glass as the level within the glass rises). This is then repeated, with any remaining liquid ingredients, using a clean teaspoon with each new layer.

the right ice

The topic of ice is a broad one within the world of mixology. Get the ice right and you have the foundations of a great cocktail; but get it wrong, and it can demote a great drink to just average.

The job of ice is two-fold: during the mixing process, it helps to chill and actively mixes the ingredients, and once the drink is served, it works to keep the cocktail cold and keeps further dilution to a minimum. There are three different types of ice used in the cocktail recipes that follow, and each has distinctive properties that complement the styles and flavors within a drink.

> **Cubed ice:** This is generally used to finish a drink. It's important to remember that the more ice you have in your glass, the colder it will keep the drink, the slower the ice will melt, and so the less your finished cocktail will be diluted. Ice cubes can be made in your freezer at home with a standard ice cube tray. Plus the whole cubes can be broken down and used to make cracked and crushed ice as necessary.

> **Cracked ice:** This is smaller than full ice cubes and is generally used in a shaker to chill the liquid ingredients before straining. To create cracked ice from whole ice cubes, simply wrap in a clean, dry dish towel and give them a gentle knock with a rolling pin or other implement. You should aim to break or crack the ice cube into pieces no smaller than a halved cube.

> **Crushed ice:** This is perfect for blended drinks because it speeds up the mixing process and rapidly freezes the whole concoction. In some drinks, it is preferable to use cracked or crushed ice, because it allows us to pack the glass with the maximum amount of ice (cubes leave greater gaps). To create crushed ice from whole ice cubes, wrap in a dish towel and break with repeated, moderate knocks with a rolling pin or other implement. You should aim to break the ice cubes into very small pieces of a consistent size.

>1 >2 >3

pick your glassware

The selection of the right glassware is an often underestimated part of the cocktail-making process. For some mixologists the glass is actually considered to be as important as the ingredients themselves—the shape, style, and size all have an impact on the visual perception and overall enjoyment of the drink. As a consequence, we have all come to associate drinks with specific glassware—consider the Cosmopolitan, which is now synonymous with a stylish yet simple Martini glass, or a Long Island Iced Tea, which surely could be served in nothing but a tall, ice-filled glass.

Conversely, serving a cocktail in the wrong glass, or one generally associated with a different drink, will detract from the presentation and experience. For this reason, each of the glasses recommended in this book has been chosen to enhance the cocktail that they have been assigned to.

final flourishes

Many consider the garnish to be the defining element of a cocktail. In some cases, the garnish can be synonymous with the drink itself—think of the Piña Colada with its obligatory pineapple slice. As a result, they are often a vital ingredient; however, in other cases a garnish appears primarily for aesthetics.

There are a number of basic guidelines that are used for adding the final flourishes to a drink, but ultimately the way in which we may choose to garnish a cocktail is often up to the imagination and artistic flair of the mixologist. One of the simplest rules to follow is to match the garnish to the featured flavors. In this book, we have recommended some simple garnishes to go with the recipes, but if you want to have some fun, throw the rule book away and experiment with creating your own. Think of your cocktail as a blank canvas.

Enjoy your drinks, but don't make yourself ill by overindulging, and always follow the drinking laws! Remember—to get the maximum pleasure out of your cocktails, follow the recipes in this book, practice and use well-honed mixing methods, choose the right glass, garnish with care, and above all, enjoy!

Paul Martin is a multi-award-winning cocktail mixologist, author of numerous cocktail books, and twice Guinness World Record holder (having mixed 196 different cocktails, one at a time, in 60 minutes). During the last ten years, he has earned a reputation as one of the most inspirational mentors in the drink industry, running mixology courses for countless brands. Paul has also appeared on numerous television programs in his capacity as a cocktail expert.

>4 >5 >6

classic cocktails

martini

serves 1

ingredients
4½ oz. gin
1 tsp. dry vermouth,
  or to taste
cocktail olive,
  to decorate

>1 Put 4–6 cracked ice cubes into a cocktail shaker.

>2 Pour the gin and vermouth over the ice.

16

>3 Shake until well frosted. Strain into a chilled cocktail glass.

>4 Decorate with the olive.

Serve immediately.

margarita

serves 1

ingredients
2 lime wedges
kosher salt
4½ oz. white tequila
1½ oz. triple sec or
 Cointreau
3 oz. lime juice

>1 Rub the rim of a chilled cocktail glass with one of the lime wedges.

>2 Dip in a saucer of kosher salt.

>3 Put 4–6 cracked ice cubes into a cocktail shaker. Pour the tequila, triple sec, and lime juice over the ice. Shake vigorously until frosted. Strain into the glass.

Serve immediately.

>4 Decorate with the remaining lime wedge.

club mojito

serves 1

ingredients

1 tsp. sugar syrup
6 fresh mint leaves,
  plus extra to
  decorate
juice of ½ lime
3 oz. Jamaican rum
club soda
dash Angostura
  bitters

>1 Put the sugar syrup, mint leaves, and lime juice into an old-fashioned glass.

>2 Muddle the mint leaves, then fill the glass halfway with cracked ice and pour over the rum

>3 Fill up with club soda.

>4 Finish with the Angostura bitters and decorate with the remaining mint leaves.

Serve immediately.

bellini

serves 1

ingredients
1 lemon wedge
superfine sugar
1½ oz. peach juice
4½ oz. champagne,
  chilled

>1 Rub the rim of a chilled champagne flute with the lemon wedge.

>2 Put the sugar in a saucer, then dip the rim of the flute in it to frost.

>3 Pour the peach juice into the flute.

Serve immediately.

>4 Fill up with the champagne.

bloody mary

serves 1

ingredients
dash Tabasco
 sauce
dash Worcestershire
 sauce
3 oz. vodka
1 cup tomato juice
juice of ½ lemon
pinch celery salt
pinch cayenne
 pepper
celery stalk and
 lemon slice,
 to decorate

>**1** Put 4–6 cracked ice cubes into a cocktail shaker. Add the dash of Tabasco sauce and Worcestershire sauce over the ice.

>**2** Add the vodka and tomato juice.

Serve immediately.

>3 Add the lemon juice and shake vigorously until well frosted.

>4 Strain into a tall, chilled glass, add the celery salt and cayenne pepper, and decorate with the celery stalk and lemon slice.

manhattan

serves 1

ingredients
dash Angostura
  bitters
4½ oz. rye whiskey
1½ oz. sweet
  vermouth
cocktail cherry,
  to decorate

>1 Put 4–6 cracked ice cubes
into a cocktail shaker.

>2 Pour the liquid ingredients over
the ice.

>3 Shake vigorously until well frosted.

Serve immediately.

>4 Strain into a chilled cocktail glass and decorate with the cherry.

cosmopolitan

serves 1

ingredients
3 oz. vodka
1½ oz. triple sec
1½ oz. lime juice
1½ oz. cranberry
  juice
orange peel strip,
  to decorate

>1 Put 4–6 cracked ice cubes into a cocktail shaker.

>2 Pour the liquid ingredients over the ice.

Serve immediately.

>3 Shake vigorously until well frosted.

>4 Strain into a chilled cocktail glass and decorate with the orange peel.

long island iced tea

serves 1

ingredients
3 oz. vodka
1½ oz. gin
1½ oz. white tequila
1½ oz. white rum
2 tsp. white crème
  de menthe
3 oz. lemon juice
1 tsp. superfine
  sugar
cola
lime wedge,
  to decorate

>1 Put 4–6 cracked ice cubes into a cocktail shaker. Pour all the liquid ingredients except the cola over the ice, add the sugar, and shake vigorously until well frosted.

>2 Fill a tall glass halfway with cracked ice and strain the cocktail over the ice.

> **>3** Fill up with cola.

Serve immediately.

> **>4** Decorate with the lime wedge.

sidecar

serves 1

ingredients
3 oz. brandy
1½ oz. triple sec
1½ oz. lemon juice
1 orange

>1 Put 4–6 cracked ice cubes into a cocktail shaker. Pour the liquid ingredients over the ice.

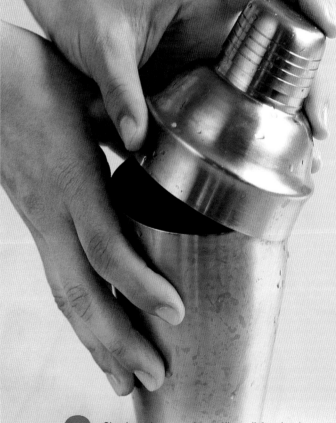

>2 Shake vigorously until well frosted.

>3 Peel a strip of orange zest to use for decoration.

>4 Strain into a chilled cocktail glass and decorate with the orange peel.

Serve immediately.

singapore sling

serves 1

ingredients
3 oz. gin
1½ oz. cherry
  brandy
1½ oz. lemon juice
1 tsp. grenadine
club soda
lime peel strips and
  cocktail cherries,
  to decorate

>1 Put 4–6 cracked ice cubes into a cocktail shaker, then pour the gin over the ice.

>2 Add the cherry brandy, lemon juice, and grenadine and shake vigorously until well frosted.

>3 Fill a chilled glass halfway with cracked ice and strain over the cocktail.

>4 Fill up with club soda and decorate with the lime peel and cherries.

Serve immediately.

old-fashioned

serves 1

ingredients
1 sugar cube
dash of Angostura
  bitters
1 tsp. water
3 oz. bourbon or rye
  whiskey
lemon peel twist,
  to decorate

>1 Place the sugar cube in a small, chilled old-fashioned glass.

>2 Add the Angostura bitters and water. Stir until the sugar has dissolved.

>3 Pour in the bourbon and stir.

>4 Add 4–6 cracked ice cubes and decorate with the lemon peel.

Serve immediately.

daiquiri

serves 1

ingredients
3 oz. white rum
¾ tsp. lime juice
½ tsp. superfine
  sugar, dissolved
  in 1 tbsp. boiling
  water
lime wedge,
  to decorate

>1 Put 4–6 cracked ice cubes into a cocktail shaker.

>2 Pour the rum, lime juice, and sugar water over the ice.

38

>3 Shake vigorously until well frosted.

Serve immediately.

>4 Strain into a chilled cocktail glass and decorate with a wedge of lime.

39

moscow mule

serves 1

ingredients
3 oz. vodka
1½ oz. lime juice
ginger beer
lime wedge,
  to decorate

>1 Put 4–6 cracked ice cubes into a cocktail shaker.

>2 Pour the vodka and lime juice over the ice and shake vigorously until well frosted.

>3 Fill a chilled glass halfway with cracked ice and strain the cocktail over the ice.

>4 Fill up with ginger beer and decorate with the lime wedge.

Serve immediately.

hurricane

serves 1

ingredients
6 oz. dark rum
1½ oz. lemon juice
3 oz. orange and
 passion fruit juice
club soda
orange slices and
 cocktail cherries,
 to decorate

>1 Put 4–6 cracked ice cubes
into a cocktail shaker.

>2 Add the rum, lemon juice, and
orange and passion fruit juice, and
shake until well combined.

Serve immediately.

>3 Pour the cocktail into a tall, chilled glass.

>4 Fill up with club soda and decorate with the orange slices and cherries.

zombie

serves 1

ingredients
3 oz. dark rum
3 oz. white rum
1½ oz. golden rum
1½ oz. triple sec
1½ oz. lime juice
1½ oz. orange juice
1½ oz. pineapple
 juice
1½ oz. guava juice
1 tbsp. grenadine
1 tbsp. orgeat syrup
1 tsp. Pernod
fresh mint sprig and
 pineapple wedge,
 to decorate

>1 Put 4–6 crushed ice cubes into a cocktail shaker.

>2 Pour the liquid ingredients over the ice and shake vigorously until well frosted.

>3 Pour the cocktail into a chilled glass.

>4 Decorate with the fresh mint and the pineapple wedge.

Serve immediately.

tom collins

serves 1

ingredients
4½ oz. gin
3 oz. lemon juice
1½ tbsp. sugar
 syrup
club soda
lemon slice,
 to decorate

>1 Put 4–6 cracked ice cubes into a cocktail shaker.

>2 Pour the gin, lemon juice, and sugar syrup over the ice and shake vigorously until well frosted.

>3 Strain into a chilled Collins glass.

>4 Fill up with club soda and decorate with the lemon slice.

Serve immediately.

WOO-WOO

serves 1

ingredients
¾ cup cranberry
 juice
3 oz. vodka
3 oz. peach
 schnapps

 >1 Fill a chilled cocktail glass halfway with crushed ice.

>2 Pour the cranberry juice over the ice.

>**3** Add the vodka and peach schnapps.

Serve immediately.

>**4** Stir well to mix.

harvey wallbanger

serves 1

ingredients
4½ oz. vodka
1½ cups orange
  juice
2 tsp. Galliano
cocktail cherry and
  orange slice,
  to decorate

>1 Fill a tall glass halfway with cracked ice.

>2 Pour the vodka and orange juice over the ice.

> **>3** Float the Galliano on top.

> **>4** Decorate with the cherry and the orange slice.

Serve immediately.

screwdriver

serves 1

ingredients
3 oz. vodka
orange juice
orange slice,
  to decorate

>**1** Fill a tall, chilled glass with cracked ice. Pour the vodka over the ice.

>**2** Fill up with orange juice.

> **>3** Stir well to mix.

> **>4** Decorate with the orange slice.

Serve immediately.

piña colada

serves 1

ingredients
4–6 crushed ice
 cubes
3 oz. white rum
1½ oz. dark rum
¾ cup pineapple
 juice
3 oz. cream of
 coconut
cocktail cherry and
 pineapple wedge,
 to decorate

>1 Put the ice in a blender and pour in the white rum, dark rum, and pineapple juice.

>2 Add the cream of coconut, then blend the mixture until smooth.

Serve immediately.

>**3** Pour, without straining, into a chilled glass.

>**4** Decorate with the cocktail cherry and the pineapple wedge.

caipirinha

serves 1

ingredients
6 lime wedges
2 tsp. granulated
  sugar
4½ oz. cachaça

>1 Put the lime wedges in a chilled old-fashioned glass.

>2 Add the sugar.

>3 Muddle the lime wedges, then pour over the cachaça.

>4 Fill the glass with cracked ice and stir well.

Serve immediately.

57

mai tai

serves 1

ingredients
3 oz. white rum
3 oz. dark rum
1½ oz. orange
 curaçao
1½ oz. lime juice
1 tbsp. orgeat syrup
1 tbsp. grenadine

to decorate
pineapple wedge
pineapple leaves
cocktail cherry
orange peel twist

>1 Put 4–6 cracked ice cubes into a cocktail shaker. Pour the white rum, dark rum, curaçao, lime juice, orgeat syrup, and grenadine over the ice.

>2 Shake vigorously until well frosted and strain into a chilled glass.

>3 De............ ....eapple wedge.

>4 Decor......... ....ple leaves,
cocktail ....nge peel.

Serve immediately.

mimosa

serves 1

ingredients
1 passion fruit
1½ tbsp. orange
  curaçao
champagne,
  chilled
star fruit
  (carambola)
  slice, to decorate

>1 Put 4–6 cracked ice cubes
into a cocktail shaker.

>2 Scoop out the passion fruit flesh
into the shaker.

>3 Add the curaçao and shake until frosted.

Serve immediately.

>4 Strain into a chilled champagne flute, fill up with champagne, and decorate with the star fruit slice.

61

tequila sunrise

serves 1

ingredients
3 oz. silver tequila
orange juice
1½ oz. grenadine
orange slice and
 cocktail cherry,
 to decorate

>**1** Put 4–6 cracked ice cubes into a chilled highball glass. Pour the tequila over the ice.

>**2** Fill up with orange juice.

Serve immediately.

>3 Stir well to mix.

>4 Slowly pour the grenadine over the orange juice mixture. Decorate with the orange slice and cocktail cherry.

tequila slammer

serves 1

ingredients
1½ oz. silver tequila,
 chilled
juice of ½ lemon
sparkling wine, chilled

>1 Put the tequila into a chilled glass.

>2 Add the lemon juice.

>**3** Fill up with sparkling wine.

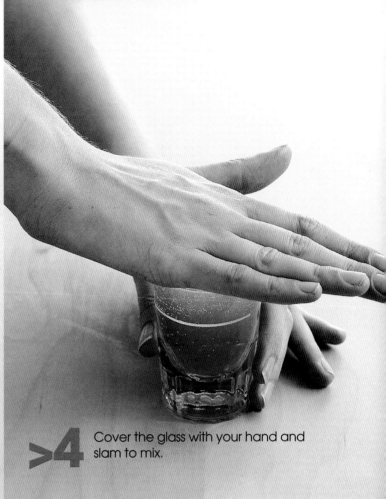

>**4** Cover the glass with your hand and slam to mix.

Serve immediately.

vodka & gin cocktails

apple martini

serves 1

ingredients
1½ oz. vodka
1½ oz. sour apple
 schnapps
1½ oz. apple juice
apple wedge,
 to decorate

>1 Put 4–6 cracked ice cubes into a cocktail shaker.

>2 Pour in the vodka, schnapps, and apple juice.

Serve immediately.

>3 Shake vigorously until well frosted.

>4 Strain into a chilled cocktail glass and decorate with the apple wedge.

metropolitan

serves 1

ingredients
1 lemon wedge
1 tbsp. superfine
  sugar
1½ tbsp. vodka
1½ tbsp. framboise
  liqueur
1½ tbsp. cranberry
  juice
1½ tbsp. orange
  juice

>1 Rub the rim of a cocktail glass with the lemon wedge.

>2 Dip into the sugar to coat.

Serve immediately.

>3 Put 4–6 cracked ice cubes into a cocktail shaker and pour the liquid ingredients over the ice.

>4 Cover and shake, until the outside of the shaker is frosted. Strain into the glass.

fuzzy navel

serves 1

ingredients
3 oz. vodka
1½ oz. peach
  schnapps
1 cup orange juice

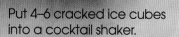 **>1** Put 4–6 cracked ice cubes into a cocktail shaker.

>2 Pour the liquid ingredients over the ice.

Serve immediately.

>**3** Shake vigorously until well frosted.

>**4** Strain into a chilled cocktail glass.

aurora borealis

serves 1

ingredients

1½ oz. grappa or
   vodka, chilled
1½ oz. green
   Chartreuse, chilled
1½ tbsp. orange
   curaçao, chilled
few drops crème
   de cassis, chilled

>1 Pour the grappa slowly over the back of a spoon around one side of a well chilled shot glass.

>2 Gently pour the Chartreuse around the other side.

>3 Pour the curaçao gently into the middle.

>4 Add a few drops of crème de cassis.

Serve immediately.

peartini

serves 1

ingredients
1 tsp. superfine sugar
pinch ground
  cinnamon
1 lemon wedge
1½ oz. vodka
1½ oz. pear brandy

>1 Mix the sugar and cinnamon in a saucer.

>2 Rub the rim of a cocktail glass with the lemon wedge.

Serve immediately.

>3 Dip into the sugar-and-cinnamon mixture to coat.

>4 Put 4–6 cracked ice cubes into a cocktail shaker and pour in the vodka and pear brandy. Stir well and strain into the glass.

salty dog

serves 1

ingredients
1 tbsp. granulated
  sugar
1 tbsp. kosher salt
1 lime wedge
3 oz. vodka
grapefruit juice

>1 Mix the sugar and salt
in a saucer.

>2 Rub the rim of a chilled cocktail
glass with the lime wedge.

>3 Dip into the sugar-and-salt mixture to coat.

Serve immediately.

>4 Fill the glass with cracked ice and pour the vodka over the ice. Fill up with the grapefruit juice and stir.

sex on the beach

serves 1

ingredients

1½ oz. peach
  schnapps
1½ oz. vodka
3 oz. fresh orange
  juice
4½ oz. cranberry and
  peach juice
dash lemon juice
orange peel twist,
  to decorate

>1 Put 4–6 cracked ice cubes into a cocktail shaker. Pour the schnapps, vodka, orange juice, and cranberry and peach juice over the ice

>2 Shake until well frosted.

> **3** Strain into a glass filled with crushed ice.

> **4** Squeeze the lemon juice over the drink and decorate with the orange peel.

Serve immediately.

a sloe kiss

serves 1

ingredients
1½ tbsp. sloe gin
1½ tbsp. Southern
 Comfort
1½ oz. vodka
1 tsp. amaretto
splash of Galliano
orange juice
orange peel twist,
 to decorate

>1 Put 4–6 cracked ice cubes into a cocktail shaker, pour in the sloe gin, Southern Comfort, vodka, and amaretto, and shake until well frosted.

>2 Strain into a long, chilled glass filled with cracked ice.

>3 Splash on the Galliano.

>4 Fill up with orange juice and decorate with the orange peel.

Serve immediately.

kamikaze

serves 1

ingredients
1½ oz. vodka
1½ oz. triple sec
1½ tbsp. fresh
  lime juice
1½ tbsp. fresh
  lemon juice
dry white wine,
  chilled
cucumber and lime
  slices, to decorate

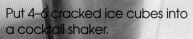

>1 Put 4–6 cracked ice cubes into a cocktail shaker.

>2 Pour in the vodka, triple sec, lime juice, and lemon juice and shake until well frosted.

>3 Strain into a chilled glass.

>4 Fill up with wine and decorate with the cucumber and lime slices.

Serve immediately.

seabreeze

serves 1

ingredients
1⅓ oz. vodka
1½ tbsp. cranberry
 juice
pink grapefruit juice

>1 Put 4–6 cracked ice cubes into a cocktail shaker.

>2 Pour in the vodka and cranberry juice and shake until frosted.

> **3** Strain into a chilled glass.

> **4** Fill up with pink grapefruit juice.

Serve immediately.

mimi

serves 1

ingredients
3 oz. vodka
1½ tbsp. cream of
  coconut
3 oz. pineapple
  juice
4–6 crushed ice
  cubes
fresh pineapple
  slice, to decorate

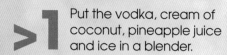**1** Put the vodka, cream of
coconut, pineapple juice
and ice in a blender.

2 Blend for a few seconds,
until frothy.

> **3** Pour into a chilled cocktail glass.

Serve immediately.

> **4** Decorate with a slice of pineapple.

cranberry collins

serves 1

ingredients
3 oz. vodka
2 tbsp. elderflower
 syrup
4½ oz. cranberry juice
club soda
lime slice and lime peel
 twist, to decorate

>1 Put 4–6 cracked ice cubes into a cocktail shaker.

>2 Pour in the vodka, elderflower syrup, and cranberry juice and shake until well frosted.

>3 Strain into a Collins glass filled with cracked ice.

>4 Fill up with club soda and decorate with the lime slice and peel.

Serve immediately.

flying grasshopper

serves 1

ingredients
1½ oz. vodka
1½ oz. green crème
 de menthe
1½ oz. crème de
 cacao
fresh mint,
 to decorate

>1 Put 4–6 cracked ice cubes into a mixing glass.

>2 Pour in the vodka, crème de menthe, and crème de cacao.

> **>3** Stir well.

Serve immediately.

> **>4** Strain into a chilled cocktail glass and decorate with a sprig of fresh mint.

vodka espresso

serves 1

ingredients

3 oz. espresso or
  other strong black
  coffee, cooled
1½ oz. vodka
2 tsp. superfine
  sugar
1½ oz. Amarula

>1 Put 4–6 cracked ice cubes into a cocktail shaker.

>2 Pour in the coffee and vodka, add the sugar, and shake vigorously until well frosted.

Serve immediately.

>3 Strain into a chilled cocktail glass.

>4 Float the Amarula on top.

95

belle collins

serves 1

ingredients
2 fresh mint sprigs,
  plus extra to
  decorate
3 oz. gin
1½ oz. lemon juice
1 tsp. sugar syrup
sparkling water

>1 Muddle the mint sprigs.

>2 Place the mint in a chilled glass and pour in the gin, lemon juice, and sugar syrup.

>3 Add 4–6 crushed ice cubes to the glass.

>4 Fill up with sparkling water, stir gently, and decorate with more fresh mint.

Serve immediately.

teardrop

serves 1

ingredients
3 oz. apricot nectar
  or peach nectar
1½ oz. gin
1½ oz. light cream
1½ tbsp. strawberry
  syrup
fresh strawberry
  and peach slices,
  to decorate

>1 Put the apricot nectar into a blender.

>2 Pour in the gin and cream. Blend for 5–10 seconds, until thick and frothy.

Serve immediately.

>3 Pour into a tall glass filled with crushed ice.

>4 Splash the strawberry syrup on top and decorate with the strawberry and peach slices.

bleu bleu bleu

serves 1

ingredients
1½ oz. gin
1½ oz. vodka
1½ oz. tequila
1½ oz. fresh lemon
  juice
2 dashes egg white
1½ oz. blue
  curaçao
club soda
lemon slice,
  to decorate

>**1** Put crushed ice from
4–6 crushed ice cubes into
a cocktail shaker.

>**2** Add the gin, vodka, tequila, lemon
juice, and egg white.

>3 Add the curaçao and shake until frosted.

>4 Strain the cocktail into a tall glass filled with crushed ice and top up with club soda. Decorate with a lemon slice.

Serve immediately.

gin rickey
serves 1

ingredients
3 oz. gin
1½ oz. lime juice
club soda
lemon slice,
  to decorate

>**1** Fill a chilled highball glass or goblet with cracked ice.

>**2** Pour in the gin and lime juice.

Serve immediately.

>3 Fill up with club soda.

>4 Stir gently to mix and decorate with a lemon slice.

blue blooded

serves 1

ingredients

4–6 crushed ice
cubes
1½ oz. gin
1½ oz. passion fruit
nectar
4 cubes melon or
mango
1–2 tsp. blue
curaçao

 Put the ice, gin, and passion fruit
nectar into a blender.

>**2** Add the melon cubes and blend
until smooth and frosted.

>3 Pour into a tall, chilled glass filled with crushed ice.

>4 Top with the curaçao.

daisy

serves 1

ingredients
4½ oz. gin
1½ oz. lemon juice
1 tbsp. grenadine
1 tbsp. sugar syrup
club soda
orange wedge,
  to decorate

>1 Put 4–6 cracked ice cubes into a cocktail shaker.

>2 Pour in the gin, lemon juice, grenadine, and sugar syrup and shake vigorously until well frosted.

> **>3** Strain the cocktail into a chilled highball glass.

> **>4** Fill up with club soda, stir gently, and decorate with the orange wedge.

Serve immediately.

pink pussycat

serves 1

ingredients
dash grenadine
3 oz. gin
pineapple juice
pineapple slice,
  to decorate

>1 Fill a chilled glass halfway with cracked ice.

>2 Dash the grenadine over the ice.

>**3** Pour in the gin.

>**4** Fill up with pineapple juice and decorate with the pineapple slice.

Serve immediately.

bloodhound

serves 1

ingredients
3 oz. gin
1½ oz. sweet
  vermouth
1½ oz. dry
  vermouth
3 strawberries, plus
  one to decorate
4–6 crushed ice
  cubes

>1 Put the gin, sweet vermouth, dry vermouth, and strawberries into a blender.

>2 Add the ice.

>3 Blend until smooth.

Serve immediately.

>4 Pour into a chilled cocktail glass and decorate with the remaining strawberry.

dirty martini

serves 1

ingredients
4½ oz. gin
1½ oz. dry
  vermouth
1½ tbsp. brine
  (from jar of
  cocktail olives)
cocktail olive,
  to decorate

>1 Put 4–6 cracked ice cubes into a cocktail shaker.

>2 Pour in the gin, vermouth, and brine.

Serve immediately.

>3 Shake vigorously until well frosted.

>4 Strain into a chilled cocktail glass and decorate with the olive.

dry martini

serves 1

ingredients
1½ oz. London
   dry gin
dash dry vermouth
cocktail olive,
   to decorate

>**1** Put 4–6 cracked ice cubes into a cocktail shaker.

>**2** Pour in the gin and vermouth.

>3 Shake until well frosted.

Serve immediately.

>4 Strain into a chilled glass and decorate with the olive.

alexander

serves 1

ingredients
1½ oz. gin
1½ oz. crème de
  cacao
1½ oz. light cream
freshly grated
  nutmeg,
  to decorate

>1 Put 4–6 cracked ice cubes into a cocktail shaker.

>2 Pour in the gin, crème de cacao, and cream and shake vigorously until well frosted.

>3 Strain into a chilled cocktail glass.

>4 Sprinkle over the grated nutmeg.

Serve immediately.

whiskey & rum cocktails

whiskey sour

serves 1

ingredients

3 oz. blended whiskey
1½ oz. lime juice
1 tbsp. confectioners'
   sugar or sugar syrup
lime slice and
   cocktail cherry,
   to decorate

>1 Put 4–6 cracked ice cubes into a cocktail shaker. Pour over the whiskey.

>2 Pour over the lime juice.

>3 Add the sugar and shake well.

>4 Strain into a cocktail glass and decorate with the slice of lime and a cherry.

mint julep

serves 1

ingredients

1 fresh mint sprig,
 plus extra to
 decorate
1 tbsp. sugar syrup
4½ oz. bourbon

>1 Strip the leaves from the mint sprig and put in a small, chilled glass.

>2 Crush the mint leaves and pour in the sugar syrup.

>**3** Fill the glass halfway with cracked ice and stir.

>**4** Add the bourbon and decorate with the remaining mint sprig.

Serve immediately.

french kiss

serves 1

ingredients
3 oz. bourbon
1½ oz. apricot liqueur
2 tsp. grenadine
1 tsp. lemon juice

>1 Put 4–6 cracked ice cubes into a cocktail shaker.

>2 Pour the liquid ingredients over the ice.

Serve immediately.

>3 Shake vigorously until well frosted.

>4 Strain into a chilled cocktail glass.

miami beach

serves 1

ingredients
3 oz. Scotch whisky
1⅓ oz. dry
  vermouth
3 oz. pink grapefruit
  juice
orange peel strip,
  to decorate

>1 Put 4–6 cracked ice cubes into a cocktail shaker.

>2 Pour in the whisky, vermouth, and grapefruit juice.

Serve immediately.

>3 Shake vigorously until well frosted. Strain into a chilled cocktail glass.

>4 Decorate with the orange peel strip.

highland fling

serves 1

ingredients
dash of Angostura
 bitters
3 oz. Scotch whisky
1½ oz. sweet
 vermouth
cocktail olive,
 to decorate

>1 Put 4–6 cracked ice cubes into a mixing glass.

>2 Pour the Angostura bitters over the ice.

>3 Pour in the whisky and vermouth and stir well to mix.

>4 Strain into a chilled glass and decorate with the olive.

Serve immediately.

whiskey sling

serves 1

ingredients

1 tsp. confectioners'
  sugar
1½ oz. lemon juice
1 tsp. water
3 oz. blended
  whiskey
orange wedge,
  to decorate

>1 Put the sugar into a mixing glass.

>2 Add the lemon juice and water and stir until the sugar has dissolved.

>**3** Pour in the whiskey and stir to mix.

>**4** Fill a small, chilled glass halfway with cracked ice and strain the cocktail over it. Decorate with the orange wedge.

Serve immediately.

queen of memphis

serves 1

ingredients
3 oz. bourbon
1½ oz. Midori
1½ oz. peach juice
dash maraschino
  liqueur
melon wedge,
  to decorate

>1 Put 4-6 cracked ice cubes into a cocktail shaker.

>2 Pour in the bourbon, Midori, peach juice, and maraschino. Shake vigorously until well frosted.

Serve immediately.

>**3** Strain into a chilled cocktail glass.

>**4** Decorate with the melon wedge.

whiskey rickey

serves 1

ingredients
3 oz. whiskey
1½ oz. lime juice
club soda
lime slice, to
  decorate

>1 Put 4–6 crushed ice cubes
into a chilled highball glass.

>2 Pour the whiskey and lime juice
over the ice.

>**3** Fill up with club soda.

Serve immediately.

>**4** Stir gently to mix and decorate with the lime slice.

klondike cooler

serves 1

ingredients
½ tsp.
  confectioners'
  sugar
1½ oz. ginger ale
3 oz. blended
  whiskey
sparkling water
lemon peel twist,
  to decorate

>1 Put the sugar into a tall, chilled glass and add the ginger ale. Stir until the sugar has dissolved.

>2 Fill the glass with cracked ice.

>**3** Pour the whiskey over the ice.

>**4** Fill up with sparkling water. Stir gently and decorate with the lemon peel.

Serve immediately.

boston sour

serves 1

ingredients

1½ oz. lemon juice
  or lime juice
3 oz. blended
  whiskey
1 tsp. sugar syrup
1 egg white
lemon slice and
  cocktail cherry,
  to decorate

>1 Put 4–6 cracked ice cubes into a cocktail shaker.

>2 Pour in the lemon juice, whiskey, and sugar syrup.

138

Serve immediately.

>3 Add the egg white.

>4 Shake until chilled. Strain into a cocktail glass and decorate with the lemon slice and a cocktail cherry.

whiskey sangaree

serves 1

ingredients
3 oz. bourbon
1 tsp. sugar syrup
club soda
1 tbsp. ruby port
freshly grated
  nutmeg, to
  decorate

>1 Put 4–6 cracked ice cubes into a chilled glass.

>2 Pour the bourbon and sugar syrup over the ice.

>3 Fill up with club soda.

>4 Stir gently to mix, then float the port on top. Sprinkle with some of the grated nutmeg.

Serve immediately.

shamrock

serves 1

ingredients
1½ oz. Irish whiskey
1½ oz. dry
   vermouth
3 dashes green
   Chartreuse
3 dashes crème
   de menthe

>1 Put 4–6 cracked ice cubes into a mixing glass.

>2 Pour the whiskey, vermouth, and Chartreuse over the ice.

Serve immediately.

>**3** Stir until well frosted.

>**4** Strain into a chilled cocktail glass, pour in the crème de menthe, and stir.

bourbon milk punch

serves 1

ingredients
3 oz. bourbon
4½ oz. milk
dash vanilla extract
1 tsp. honey
freshly grated
  nutmeg, to
  decorate

>1 Put 4–6 cracked ice cubes into a cocktail shaker.

>2 Pour the bourbon, milk, and vanilla extract over the ice.

>3 Add the honey and shake until well frosted.

>4 Strain into a chilled glass. Sprinkle with the grated nutmeg.

Serve immediately.

cuba libre

serves 1

ingredients
3 oz. white rum
cola
lime wedge,
  to decorate

>1 Fill a highball glass halfway with cracked ice.

>2 Pour the rum over the ice.

Serve immediately.

>3 Fill up with cola.

>4 Stir gently to mix and decorate with the lime wedge.

mellow mule

serves 1

ingredients
3 oz. white rum
1½ oz. dark rum
1½ oz. golden rum
1½ oz. falernum
   (wine-based ginger
   syrup)
1½ oz. lime juice
ginger beer
pineapple wedges
   and preserved
   ginger, to decorate

>1 Put 4–6 cracked ice cubes into a cocktail shaker.

>2 Pour in the white rum, dark rum, golden rum, falernum, and lime juice and shake vigorously until well frosted.

> **3** Strain the cocktail into a tall, chilled glass.

> **4** Fill up with ginger beer and decorate with the pineapple wedges and ginger.

Serve immediately.

bajan sun

serves 1

ingredients

1½ oz. white rum
1½ oz. mandarin
  brandy
1½ oz. fresh orange
  juice
1½ oz. pineapple
  juice
splash of grenadine
fresh pineapple
  slice and a
  cocktail cherry,
  to decorate

>1 Put 4–6 crushed ice cubes into a cocktail shaker.

>2 Pour in the rum, brandy, orange juice, and pineapple juice.

150

>3 Add the grenadine and shake vigorously.

>4 Strain into a tall, chilled glass and decorate with the pineapple slice and cherry.

Serve immediately.

frozen peach daiquiri

serves 1

ingredients
4–6 crushed ice
  cubes
½ peach, peeled,
  pitted, and
  chopped
3 oz. white rum
1½ oz. lime juice
1 tsp. sugar syrup
peach slice,
  to decorate

>1 Put the ice and peach into a blender.

>2 Add the rum, lime juice, and sugar syrup and blend until slushy.

> **3** Pour into a chilled cocktail glass.

Serve immediately.

> **4** Decorate with the peach slice.

cuban special

serves 1

ingredients
3 oz. white rum
1½ oz. lime juice
1 tbsp. pineapple
 juice
1 tsp. triple sec
pineapple wedges,
 to decorate

>1 Put 4–6 cracked ice cubes into a cocktail shaker.

>2 Pour in the rum, lime juice, pineapple juice, and triple sec.

Serve immediately.

>**3** Shake vigorously until well frosted. Strain into a chilled cocktail glass.

>**4** Decorate with the pineapple wedges.

ocean breeze

serves 1

ingredients
1½ oz. white rum
1½ oz. amaretto
1½ tbsp. blue
  curaçao
1½ tbsp. pineapple
  juice
club soda

> **1** Put 4–6 cracked ice cubes into a cocktail shaker.

> **2** Pour in the white rum, amaretto, blue curaçao, and pineapple juice and shake well.

>**3** Strain into a tall, chilled glass.

>**4** Fill up with club soda.

Serve immediately.

strawberry colada

serves 1

ingredients

4–6 crushed ice
  cubes
4½ oz. golden rum
¾ cup pineapple
  juice
1½ oz. cream of
  coconut
6 strawberries
pineapple wedge,
  and halved
  strawberry, to
  decorate

>1 Put the ice into a blender.

>2 Add the rum, pineapple juice, and cream of coconut.

>3 Hull the strawberries and add to the blender. Blend until smooth.

>4 Pour, without straining, into a tall, chilled glass. Decorate with the pineapple wedge and strawberry.

Serve immediately.

plantation punch

serves 1

ingredients
3 oz. dark rum
1½ oz. Southern
 Comfort
1½ oz. lemon juice
1 tbsp. brown sugar
sparkling water
1 tbsp. ruby port

>1 Put 4–6 cracked ice cubes into a cocktail shaker. Add the rum, Southern Comfort, lemon juice, and sugar.

>2 Shake vigorously until well frosted. Strain into a tall, chilled glass.

>3 Fill up with sparkling water.

>4 Float the port on top by pouring it gently over the back of a teaspoon.

Serve immediately.

blue hawaiian

serves 1

ingredients

3 oz. Bacardi rum
1½ tbsp. blue
   curaçao
1½ oz. pineapple
   juice
1½ tbsp. cream of
   coconut
pineapple wedge,
   to decorate

> **>1** Put 4–6 crushed ice cubes into a cocktail shaker.

> **>2** Pour the liquid ingredients over the ice.

>3 Shake vigorously until well frosted. Strain into a chilled wine goblet.

>4 Decorate with the pineapple wedge.

Serve immediately.

josiah's bay float

serves 1

ingredients

3 oz. golden rum
1½ oz. Galliano
3 oz. pineapple
  juice
1½ oz. lime juice
4 tsp. sugar syrup
scooped-out
  pineapple shell,
  to serve
champagne
lime slices, lemon
  slices, and
  cocktail cherries,
  to decorate

>1 Put 4–6 cracked ice cubes into a cocktail shaker.

>2 Pour in the rum, Galliano, pineapple juice, lime juice, and sugar syrup and shake vigorously until well frosted.

>3 Strain into the pineapple shell.

>4 Fill up with champagne and stir gently. Decorate with the lime and lemon slices and cocktail cherries.

Serve immediately.

banana daiquiri

serves 1

ingredients

3 oz. white rum, chilled
1½ tbsp. triple sec, chilled
1½ tbsp. lime juice
1½ tbsp. light cream, chilled
1 tsp. sugar syrup
¼ banana, peeled and sliced
lime slice, to decorate

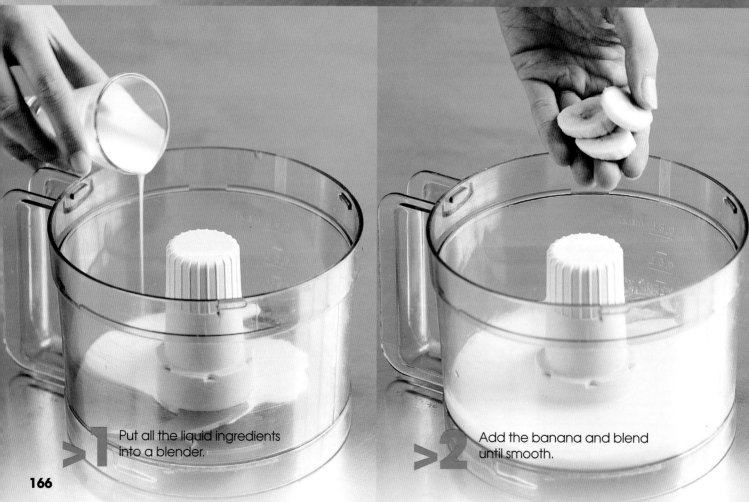

>1 Put all the liquid ingredients into a blender.

>2 Add the banana and blend until smooth.

>3 Pour, without straining, into a chilled glass.

>4 Decorate with the lime slice.

Serve immediately.

rum cooler

serves 1

ingredients

2–4 cracked ice
cubes
1½ oz. white rum
1½ oz. pineapple
juice
1 banana, peeled
and sliced
juice of 1 lime
lime peel twist,
to decorate

>1 Put the ice, rum, pineapple juice, and banana into a blender.

>2 Add the lime juice and blend for about 1 minute, or until smooth.

>**3** Fill a chilled glass with cracked ice and pour the cocktail over the ice.

>**4** Decorate with the lime peel.

Serve immediately.

bubbles,
liqueurs & virgin
cocktails

champagne cocktail

serves 1

ingredients
1 sugar cube
2 dashes Angostura
 bitters
1½ oz. brandy
champagne, chilled

>1 Place the sugar cube in the bottom of a chilled champagne flute.

>2 Add the Angostura bitters.

Serve immediately.

>3 Pour in the brandy.

>4 Fill up with champagne.

kir royale

serves 1

ingredients
few drops crème de
 cassis, or to taste
1½ tbsp. brandy
champagne, chilled
fresh mint spring,
 to decorate

>1 Put the cassis into the bottom
of a champagne flute.

>2 Add the brandy.

Serve immediately.

>**3** Fill up with champagne.

>**4** Decorate with the mint sprig.

monte carlo

serves 1

ingredients
1½ tbsp. gin
2 tsp. lemon juice
champagne or
 sparkling white
 wine, chilled
2 tsp. crème de
 menthe
fresh mint sprig,
 to decorate

> 1 Put 4–6 ice cubes into a mixing glass and pour the gin and lemon juice over the ice.

> 2 Stir until well chilled.

>3 Strain into a chilled champagne flute and fill up with champagne.

>4 Drizzle the crème de menthe over the top and decorate with the mint sprig.

flirtini

serves 1

ingredients

¼ slice fresh
  pineapple,
  chopped
1½ tbsp. chilled
  Cointreau
1½ tbsp. chilled
  vodka
1½ oz. chilled
  pineapple juice
champagne, chilled

>1 Put the pineapple into a mixing glass or pitcher.

>2 Crush the pineapple and add the Cointreau, vodka, and pineapple juice. Stir well.

Serve immediately.

>**3** Strain into a glass.

>**4** Fill up with champagne.

peacemaker

serves 4

ingredients

25 strawberries, hulled

½ small fresh pineapple, peeled and crushed

1–2 tbsp. confectioners' sugar

1½ oz. maraschino

1 cup sparkling water

1 bottle dry champagne

fresh mint leaves and sliced strawberries, to decorate

>1 Put the fruit and sugar into a large punch bowl.

>2 Add a little water and crush together.

> **>3** Add the maraschino and sparkling water and mix well.

> **>4** Top up with the champagne. Decorate with the mint leaves and strawberry slices.

Serve immediately.

champagne pick-me-up

serves 1

ingredients
3 oz. brandy
1½ oz. orange juice
1½ oz. lemon juice
dash grenadine
champagne,
  chilled

>1 Put 4–6 cracked ice cubes into a cocktail shaker.

>2 Pour in the brandy, orange juice, lemon juice, and grenadine and shake vigorously until well frosted.

>**3** Strain into a wine glass.

>**4** Fill up with champagne.

B-52

serves 1

ingredients
1½ oz. chilled dark
crème de cacao
1½ oz. chilled
Bailey's Irish
Cream
1½ oz. chilled
Grand Marnier

>1 Pour the crème de cacao into a shot glass.

>2 With a steady hand, gently pour in the Bailey's to make a second layer.

>3 Gently pour in the Grand Marnier.

>4 Cover with your hand and slam to mix or, alternatively, serve with layers intact.

Serve immediately.

185

tricolour

serves 1

ingredients

1½ oz. chilled
  red maraschino
  liqueur
1½ oz. chilled
  crème de menthe
1½ oz. chilled
  Bailey's Irish
  Cream
fresh mint leaf,
  to decorate

>1 Pour the maraschino into a chilled shot glass.

>2 Gently pour in the crème de menthe to make a second layer.

>3 Gently pour in the Bailey's Irish Cream.

>4 Decorate with the mint leaf.

Serve immediately.

rattlesnake

serves 1

ingredients

1½ oz. chilled dark
crème de cacao
1½ oz. chilled
Bailey's Irish
Cream
1½ oz. chilled
Kahlúa
cocktail cherry,
to decorate

>1 Pour the crème de cacao into a shot glass.

>2 With a steady hand, gently pour in the Bailey's Irish Cream to make a second layer.

>3 Pour in the Kahlúa to make a third layer.
Do not stir.

>4 Decorate with the cherry..

Serve immediately.

sangria

serves 6

ingredients
juice of 1 orange
juice of 1 lemon
2 tbsp.
  confectioners'
  sugar
1 orange, thinly
  sliced
1 lemon, thinly
  sliced
1 bottle chilled
  red wine
lemon-flavored
  soda, to taste

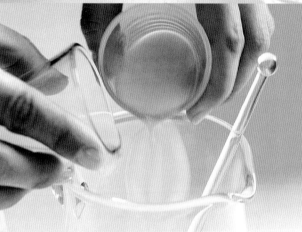

>1 Put the orange juice and lemon juice in a large pitcher. Stir.

>2 Add the sugar and stir. When the sugar has dissolved, add 4–6 cracked ice cubes.

>**3** Add the sliced fruit and the wine and marinate for 1 hour.

>**4** Add lemon-flavored soda to taste, then fill up with cracked ice.

Serve immediately.

brandy alexander

serves 1

ingredients
1 ½ oz. brandy
1 ½ oz. dark crème
de cacao
1 ½ oz. heavy
cream
freshly grated
nutmeg, to
decorate

>1 Put 4–6 cracked ice cubes into a cocktail shaker.

>2 Pour in the brandy, crème de cacao, and cream and shake vigorously until well frosted.

192

Serve immediately.

>**3** Strain into a chilled cocktail glass.

>**4** Sprinkle with the grated nutmeg.

ginger fizz

serves 1

ingredients
ginger ale
fresh mint sprigs
fresh raspberries
  and a sprig of
  mint, to decorate

>1 Put 3 ounces of ginger ale into a blender.

>2 Add a few mint sprigs and blend together.

>3 Fill a chilled highball glass two-thirds of the way with cracked ice, strain the ginger ale-and-mint mixture over the ice, and fill with more ginger ale.

>4 Decorate with raspberries and the mint sprig.

Serve immediately.

shirley temple

serves 1

ingredients
3 oz. lemon juice
1½ tbsp. grenadine
1½ tbsp. sugar syrup
ginger ale
orange slice,
 to decorate

>**1** Put 4–6 cracked ice cubes into a cocktail shaker.

>**2** Pour in the lemon juice, grenadine, and sugar syrup and shake vigorously until well frosted.

>3 Fill a chilled highball glass halfway with cracked ice, then strain the cocktail over the ice.

>4 Fill up with ginger ale and decorate with the orange slice.

Serve immediately.

mini colada

serves 1

ingredients
1 cup milk
4½ oz. cream of
    coconut
¾ cup pineapple
    juice

to decorate
pineapple cubes
pineapple leaf
cocktail cherry

>1 Put 4–6 cracked ice cubes into a cocktail shaker.

>2 Pour the milk and cream of coconut over the ice.

>3 Add the pineapple juice and shake vigorously until well frosted.

Serve immediately.

199

>4 Fill a highball glass halfway with cracked ice, strain the cocktail into it, and decorate with the pineapple cubes, pineapple leaf, and cherry.

faux kir royale

serves 1

ingredients
3 oz. raspberry
  syrup
sparkling apple
  juice, chilled

>1 Put 4–6 cracked ice cubes into a mixing glass. Pour the raspberry syrup over the ice.

>2 Stir well to mix.

Serve immediately.

>3 Strain into a chilled wine glass.

>4 Fill up with sparkling apple juice and stir.

maidenly
mimosa

serves 2

ingredients
¾ cup orange juice
¾ cup sparkling
  white grape juice
orange slice,
  to decorate

>**1** Chill two champagne flutes.

>**2** Divide the orange juice between the flutes.

Serve immediately.

> **>3** Fill up with the sparkling grape juice.

> **>4** Decorate with the orange slice.

cool collins

serves 1

ingredients

6 fresh mint leaves,
 plus extra to
 decorate
1 tsp. superfine
 sugar
3 oz. lemon juice
sparkling water
lemon slice,
 to decorate

>1 Put the mint leaves into a
chilled Collins glass.

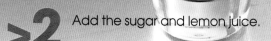

>2 Add the sugar and lemon juice.

Serve immediately.

>3 Crush the mint leaves, then stir until the sugar has dissolved.

>4 Fill the glass with cracked ice and fill up with sparkling water. Stir gently and decorate with the fresh mint and lemon slice.

prohibition punch

serves 6

ingredients
3½ cups apple
  juice
1½ cups lemon
  juice
½ cup sugar syrup
cracked ice
10 cups ginger ale
orange slices,
  to decorate

>1 Pour the apple juice into
a large pitcher.

>2 Add the lemon juice and
sugar syrup.

> **3** Add a handful of cracked ice.

> **4** Pour in the ginger ale and stir gently to mix. Pour into chilled old-fashioned glasses and decorate with the orange slices.

Serve immediately.

bright green cooler

serves 1

ingredients
4½ oz. pineapple
 juice
3 oz. lime juice
1½ oz. green
 peppermint syrup
ginger ale
cucumber strip
 and lime slice,
 to decorate

>1 Put 4–6 cracked ice cubes into a cocktail shaker.

>2 Pour in the pineapple juice, lime juice, and peppermint syrup and shake vigorously until well frosted.

Serve immediately.

>3 Fill a chilled highball glass halfway with cracked ice and strain the cocktail over it.

>4 Fill up with ginger ale and decorate with the cucumber strip and lime slice.

209

virgin mary

serves 1

ingredients
4½ oz. tomato juice
1½ oz. lemon juice
2 dashes
  Worcestershire
  sauce
1 dash Tabasco
  sauce
pinch celery salt
pepper
lemon wedge and
  celery stalk,
  to decorate

>1 Put 4–6 cracked ice cubes into a cocktail shaker. Pour the tomato juice over the ice.

>2 Add the lemon juice.

>3 Pour in the Worcestershire sauce and Tabasco sauce. Shake vigorously until well frosted.

>4 Season with the celery salt and pepper, strain into a chilled glass, and decorate with the lemon wedge and celery stalk.

Serve immediately.

mango lassi

serves 2

ingredients
1 cup milk
½ cup plain yogurt
1 tbsp. rosewater
3 tbsp. honey
1 ripe mango,
  peeled and diced
rose petals,
  to decorate
  (optional)

>**1** Pour the milk and yogurt into a blender and process until combined.

>**2** Add the rosewater and honey and process until blended.

>3 Add the mango and 4–6 crushed ice cubes and blend until smooth.

>4 Pour into two chilled glasses and decorate with the rose petals, if using.

Serve immediately.

raspberry lemonade

serves 4

ingredients
2 lemons
1 cup confectioners' sugar
1 cup raspberries
few drops vanilla extract
sparkling water
fresh mint sprigs, to decorate

> **>1** Cut the ends off the lemons, then scoop out and chop the flesh.

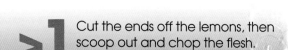

> **>2** Put the lemon flesh in a blender with the sugar, raspberries, vanilla extract, and 4–6 cracked ice cubes, then blend for 2–3 minutes.

>3 Fill four highball glasses halfway with cracked ice and strain in the lemonade.

>4 Fill up with sparkling water and decorate with the mint sprigs.

Serve immediately.

coconut cream

serves 2

ingredients
1½ cups pineapple
  juice
½ cup coconut
  milk
1 cup vanilla ice
  cream
1 cup frozen
  pineapple chunks
grated fresh
  coconut, to
  decorate

>**1** Pour the pineapple juice and coconut milk into a blender.

>**2** Add the ice cream and process until smooth.

>**3** Add the pineapple chunks and process until smooth.

>**4** Divide between two chilled glasses and decorate with the grated coconut.

Serve immediately.

heavenly days

serves 1

ingredients
3 oz. hazelnut syrup
3 oz. lemon juice
1 tsp. grenadine
sparkling water

>1 Put 4–6 cracked ice cubes into a cocktail shaker.

>2 Pour in the hazelnut syrup, lemon juice, and grenadine and shake vigorously until well frosted.

>**3** Fill a glass halfway with cracked ice and strain the cocktail over the ice.

>**4** Fill up with sparkling water and stir gently.

Serve immediately.

apple pie cream

serves 1

ingredients
4–6 crushed ice
  cubes
¾ cup apple juice
1 small scoop
  vanilla ice cream
club soda
cinnamon sugar
  and apple slice,
  to decorate

>1 Put the ice into a blender and add the apple juice and ice cream.

>2 Blend for 10–15 seconds, until frothy and frosted. Pour into a chilled glass.

>3 Fill up with club soda.

>4 Sprinkle with the cinnamon sugar and decorate with an apple slice.

Serve immediately.

Index